101 WAYS TO SAY I Love You

Romance from Afghanistan to Zambia

by
Ken Noyle

Illustrated by Ed Powers

PRICE/STERN/SLOAN
Publishers, Inc., Los Angeles

For Yoko,

at least a thousand ways

Copyright© 1983 by Ken Noyle
Illustrations Copyright© 1983 by
Price/Stern/Sloan Publishers, Inc.
Published by Price/Stern/Sloan Publishers, Inc.
410 North La Cienega Boulevard, Los Angeles, California 90048

ISBN: 0-8431-0745-6

I Love You

Three little words used by people everywhere to express an emotion as elusive as a twinkle in the eye. Mumbled with fingers crossed or breathed eloquently, "I love you" has mined more diamonds, cultivated more long-stemmed roses, mated more couples and caused more children to be conceived than any other spoken or written words.

Do lovers the world over whisper the same words? Apparently, they do. Some sibilantly, some gruntlike, some nasal, some with strange clicks and sounds, but all express this feeling with a universal intensity. I hope you'll enjoy this trip around the world with its most enduring and fascinating phrase.

A final note: I would like to express my gratitude to the many libraries, embassies and individuals who contributed words of love to these pages.

Ken Noyle

AFGHANISTAN

15,000,000 people who speak Dari say

TE ME KHOSHEJE

Those who speak Pushto/Pashto say

DOSTAT DARAM

ALBANIA

TE DASHUROJ or TE DUA

ALGERIA

125,000,000 Algerians speak Arabic and tell their loved one

ANA UHIBUKA

AMERICA

I LOVE YOU

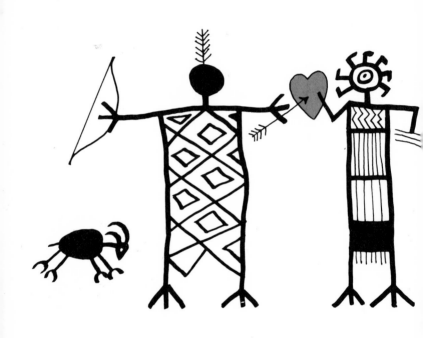

AMERICAN INDIAN

Eskimo and Inupiaq are spoken by North American Indians and people in Northwest Alaska

PIQ/PA/GI/GIP/PIN and NA/KU/A/GHI/GHIG/PIN

The message is the same, but other American Indian tribes say it differently

TS-HATL-BET-SID
SHIL-NZHU
DIA-WADZ-IS-IK

ARGENTINA

YO TE QUIERO

ARMENIA

YEZ KEZI SAD GIYISIREM GOD

AUSTRIA

ICH LIEBE DICH

BELGIUM

5,000,000 people speak Flemish and say

IK HOUD VAN JE or
IK BEMIN JE or
IK HEB JE LIEF

French is the language of an additional 75,000,000 Belgians

BHUTAN

Nepali is the language of the country

MA TANPAI LAI
MAYA GARCHU

Many languages are spoken including Sotho in which "I love you" is translated

KI-A-HU-RATA

BOTSWANA

125,000,000 people speak Portuguese to say

EU TE AMO or AMO TE

The country has many Indian tribes who speak many languages and dialects. One of the most charming expressions is used by the Borro Tribe, whose words of love can be translated as "You don't fit in my heart." This expression only exists in the negative form. The idea it conveys is that a person's love overflows his heart.

BURMA

While the sounds in Burmese are clear enough, the translation is something Westerners might ponder. Literally, their "I love you" comes out as "I think I'll go too!"

THINK-GO-CHIT-THEE

CAMBODIA

ខ្ញុំ ស្រលាញ់ អ្នក

KENYUH SHROLANG NIAK

CAPE VERDE

In a language called Crioulo, "I love you" is said

MO KÔTÂ TWA
or
UM TA AMABO

CHINA

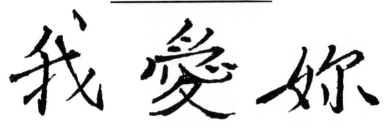

There are at least five major dialects used by the 900,000,000 Chinese. In each of them, there is a phrase that says it all

Mandarin WŌ AI NI
Amoy GUA AI DI
Cantonese NGO OI LEI
Shanghai NGOW EI NGOW
Swat WA EAI LE

COLOMBIA

In addition to Spanish, Colombians speak a language called Quechua in which they say

NUCA MUNANI

COSTA RICA

Spanish is the national language of the country, but in one of the dialects called Bribri, the phrase for "I love you" translates literally to "You cause a strong sensation in my liver!" (This group of people attribute the intellectual and emotional functions of the body to the liver.)

JA ED A SULU BE DALID

CZECHOSLOVAKIA

MILUJI TE

DENMARK

JEG ELSKER DIG

DJIBOUTI

Afar, Issa and Somali are the three languages spoken, with Somali the most popular

WON-KY-DZELA-HAI

EGYPT

انــا بحبـــك

125,000,000 Egyptians speak Arabic. Those who use the Cairo dialect say

AA HE BAA-K

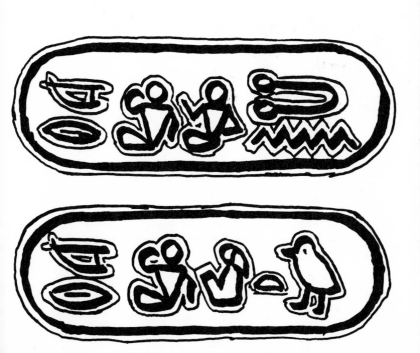

ECUADOR

Spanish is the first language, but 7,000,000 people use Quechua to say

AEHICATA MUNAI

ESTONIA

In Estonian, the population has no difficulty saying

MINA ARMASTAN SIND

FIJI

Not content with "I love you" Fijians say "A Thousand Ways to Say I Love You"

E UDOLU NA YAMEQU ENA NOQU

FINLAND

ME-NA RA-KA-STUN SI-NEW-AH

FRANCE

The French not only say JE T'AIME, they add glorious words of endearment

un petit vermisson,	poor little mite, true love
pauvre gosse	poor boy
une belle fille, une beauté	a raving beauty
ma petite mignonne (soûris)	my little sweetheart (mouse)
chouchou	favorite
mon petit lapin	little bunny
une môme bien blancée	a raving beauty
bien-aimé, soupirant, fiancé	lover, boyfriend, fiance
bien-aimée, fiancée	beloved, girlfriend, fiancee
un petit bout d'homme	
mon cher	my dear fellow
petit chou, mignon, cocotte	sweetie, babe
mon petit poulet	birdie, love-chick
poupée	baby-doll
mon trésor, mon petit coeur	my heart's desire
amour de ma vie	true love
mon sucre d'orge	sweetie pie
lumière de ma vie	light of my life
Je t'adore	I adore you

GERMANY

ICH LIEBE DICH

GHANA

Frequently the sounds of Akan, Dagbani, Ewe, Fanti, Hausa, Ga, and Twi are similar, but they are not exactly the same. In Hausa, spoken by 20,000,000 Ghanaians, "I love you" is said

NNA SON NKA

GREECE

ΣΕ ΑΓΑΠΩ

SE AGAPO

HAITI

Haitians speak French and Creole
MOUIN RINMIN OU

HAWAII
ALOHA AU IÁ OE

HUNGARY

The Magyars tend to omit the personal pronoun when they say it in Hungarian

SZERETLEK

INDIA

माझा तङ्यावर जीव जङलाय.

There are over 70 languages and dialects spoken, some by many millions of people, and some by small, more isolated groups. 125,000,000 Indians use Bengali to say "I love you"

AAMI TOMAKE BHALOBASHI

200,000,000 say it in Hindi

MEIN TUMSE PYAR KARTA HOON

Those who speak Marathi most charmingly say, "My heart is set on thee"

MA-DZHA TUJHA-VAR JI-V DZAD LA-Y

IRAN

دوستت دارم

DOOSTAT DAARAM

IRAQ

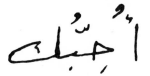

In Chaldean, a woman says to a man
EK HAY BENUCKH

And a man says to a woman
EK HAY BENACH

IRELAND

TA GRA AGAM DUIT
TAW-IM ING-RAW-LAT

ISERAEL

אני אוהב אותך

In the national tongue of Hebrew
ANI OHEV OTACH

ITALY

TI VOGLIO BENE

JAPAN

In Japanese, the loving words are said many ways

KANJI HIRANGANA
KATAKANA

JORDAN

انـــا بحبـــك

ANA BE HE-BAAK

JAMAICA

In Jamaican the words are "I man love the daughter"

AY MAN LOV DE DAHTAH

KENYA

80 languages are spoken here, prime among them Swahili

NAKUPENDA

KOREA

나는 당신을 사랑한다.

TANGSINUL JOA HAMNIDA

KUWAIT

In Arabic

ANA UHIBUKA

LAOS

ຂອຍຮັກເຈົ້າ.

KHOY HAKCHAO

LATVIA

ES YŌOS MĒ'LÓO

LITHUANIA

ASH MELU YOOS

LUXEMBOURG

In Letzebuergesch, the people of the country start out by saying

ECH SIN FRO'H MATT DER

MADAGASCAR

The official language is Malagasy

TIAKO INANAO

MALTA

INN-HOB-BOK

MONGOLIA

In New Mongolian, the words are

BU YAMA XUAPTAU

NAMBIA

German is the common language but 4,000,000 people say "I love you" in Afrikaans

ET HET JOU LIEF

NEPAL

MA TANPAI LAI MAYA GARCHU

NEW ZEALAND

In Maori, people say

AHAU AROHANUI

NORWAY

Although Nynorsk is spoken, most people use Riksmal

JEG ELSKER DEG

PAKISTAN

Of the many languages spoken, four predominate

Punjabi
MAINUN TERE NAL PIYAR HAI

Urdu
MUJE TUM SE MOHABBAT HAI

Pushto
TAH PA MA GRAN YE

Sindhi
MUNKHE TOE SAN ISHQ AMEY

PHILIPPINES

This country is made up of 7000 islands; therefore, many dialects are spoken. The national language is Tagalog, spoken in Luzon, the largest of the islands.

EE-NEE-EE-BIG/KEE-TAH

PAPUA

There are 750 vernacular dialects on this island, most of them spoken but not written.

Motu
NA LALOKAU HENIMUMU

Pidgin **MI LAIKIM YU**

Polis Motu
LAU LALOKAU HENIMU

Hiri Motu **LAU LALOKAU HENIA**

POLAND

Poles say it in Polish
YA-TSEN-KOHAM

ROMANIA

No words are wasted in Romanian
TAE JU BESK

SAUDI ARABIA

Arabic is used to say
ANA BIBBAK

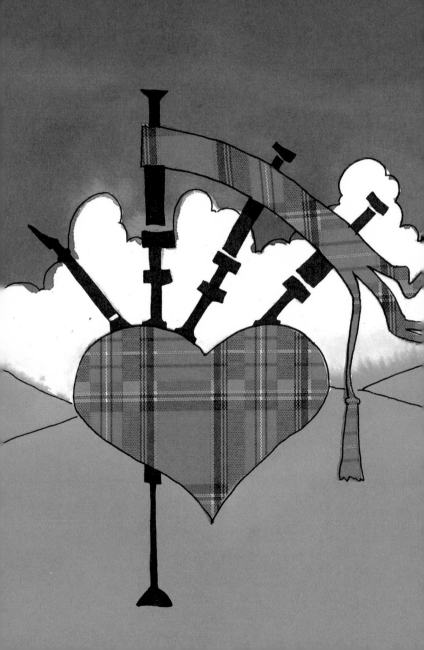

SCOTLAND

Scottish-Gaelic, a Celtic language, is the country's national tongue

THA GAOL AGAM ORT

SOMALIA

Amharic sounds this way

ENA ER WA DE SHALA

SOUTH AFRICA

South Africa is a nation of many languages including Zulu, Swazi, Tswana, Xhosa, Tsonga and Venda. In Afrikaans, "I love you" is

EK HET YOW LEEF

SPAIN

In addition to Spanish, a substantial number speak Catalan and say

T'ESTIMO MOLT

Those who speak Basque say it quite differently

NI MAITE ZAITUT

SRI LANKA

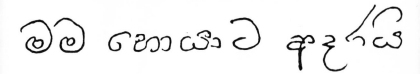

Sinhalese is the language in which the people of this country say

MAMUR HOYATA HATHERA

SWAZILAND

In Swazi, it's said

NGIYAKUTSANDZA

In Zulu, it's said

NEIYAKUTHANDA

SWITZERLAND

Three of this country's four languages are spoken internationally

German
ICH LIEBE DICH

French
JE T'AIME

Italian
TE AMO

The fourth language, Rheto Romansch, is Switzerland's own

JEU CAREZEL TEI

TANZANIA

120 different tribes speak at least 16 different dialects, including what we know as Swahili

NAKUPENDA

THAILAND

POM RUCK KOON or
CHUN RUCK KOON or
CHUN RUCK THER

TURKEY

SENI SEVIOYUM

U.S.S.R.

КАХАЮ ЦЯБЕ
or
ЛЮБЛЮ ЦЯБЕ

Russian YA TEBYA LUBLU or
YU LUBLU TEBRYA

Byelorussian
KA KHAYOO TSYABYE

Ukrainian YA TEBE KOHAYU

Georgian
ME SHEN MIKHWARKHAR

Moldavian YEU VE YUBESK

New Gagauzian
BAN SENI SEVERIM

VENEZUELA
TE QUIERO

VIET NAM
TÔI YÊU CÁC BAN

WALES

ROOEE N DU GAREE DEE

YUGOSLAVIA

How you say "I love you" depends on whether you speak

Macedonian **TE SAKAM**

Slovenian **JAZ TE MAM RAD**

Serbo-Croatian **VOLIM TE**